A Sense of Tiptoe

and other articles of faith

poems by

Karen Hayes

Holland Park Press London

Published by Holland Park Press 2020
Copyright © Karen Hayes 2020

First Edition

The moral right of Karen Hayes to be identified as the author of this work has been asserted by her in accordance with the Copyright, Designs and Patents Act of 1988.

All rights reserved. Without limiting the rights under the copyright reserved above, no part of this publication may be reproduced, stored in a retrieval system or transmitted in any form or by any means, electronic, mechanical, photocopying, recording or otherwise, without the prior permission of both the copyright owner and Holland Park Press.

British Library Cataloguing-in-Publication Data
A catalogue record for this book is available from the British Library

ISBN 978-1-907320-93-4

Cover designed by Reactive Graphics

Printed and bound by
CPI Group (UK) Ltd, Croydon CR0 4YY

www.hollandparkpress.co.uk

Dedicated to Charles Causley
1917 – 2003

Karen Hayes was inspired by iconic churches, atmospheric locations, local legends, paintings, religious artifacts and more. She often takes a mundane situation and lifts it into something more spiritual. A visit to a museum is compared to a modern-day pilgrimage, she reflects how we struggle with our doubts, fears, superstition, disease, dead and loss.

Yet far from being gloomy, there is always hope and her poems give you a warm feeling about life. The poems, therefore, not only reflect on the religious aspects of faith but also deal with faith, or lack thereof, in ourselves and our surroundings.

Contents

Definite
At the Cathedral	13
The Leper Squint	15
The Relics	17
Charmed Circle	19
Bells	21
The Prayer Book Pilgrimage	23
Oh, When the Saints	25
Galilee	28
Carvery	30

Indefinite
The Repentant Magdalene	35
Salome With the Head of John The Baptist	37
The Supper at Emmaus	39
These Thanet Skies	41
Room Thirty-One	44
Chef Jesus	48
The Twelve	50

Infinite
A Song of Parting	55
At the Crumbly Edge of Empire	57
Seventy-Nine Bench Ends	59
The Women Who Shaped the Church	61
Salvage	64
Ching Alley	66
Ralph	68
The Hurlers	70
Unborn Chicks	73
Worthy	74
Momentarily	75

DEFINITE

At the Cathedral

As if the world were ending, or beginning,
A low note throbs and builds beneath your feet.
The flat stones shudder with familiar pleasure
And, as the echoed syllables repeat
In phrases learned beyond a thousand years,
The mist around their broken silence clears.

Notes pound in rumbling chaos on the stone
And pillars weave, in thin high webs, a roof
Which shoots its hanging arches to the stars
And, wrapped in the organ's climbing sounds, a truth.
Dragging behind, unfathomable saints
Waver amongst the leads and coloured panes.

Smooth headed kings peer scowling in their crowns,
And angels swoop with wide, forbidding arms,
Their scarlet lips and medieval hair
Moulded along the balustrades like charms.
They flaunt their symbols on the wooden screen,
Chevrons of red and gold and ghastly green.

Amongst the gilded leaves and trailing vines
And tiny terra cotta buds there sleeps
An ancient dog, warm as a sunny day
Curling, quiescent at his master's feet,
As if his sculpted, hairy heart could claim
A hound's own heaven, chasing his lord's own game.

For as with all created things, it is humanity
And not the devil which lays the detail open to our sight.
Above a priestly tomb a tiny angel holds
A crowned strawberry for its occupant's delight.
John Newland of Nailheart who lies here in state
Has kept his abbot's robes immaculate.

And ordinary folk stare in relief,
Eyebrows confused, mouths open, noses chipped,
Down to the chapel floor which still vibrates.
They breathe in all its sounds with laughing lips.
And under the tiles though still within the fold
Lies someone's little son, just six years old.

The Leper Squint
St Thomas' Launceston

Down where the Tamar meets the Kensey
Where a stone bridge spans the stream,
Like starving fish, in feeding frenzy
Gather a shoal of the unclean.

And that unrealized congregation,
Neither quite dead, nor quite unborn
Crouches, a phantom population
Buzzing, like bees in queenless swarm.

Consider the blemished faithful, brothers,
Leave them stale bread and damaged fruits,
Wade ankle deep and wipe each other
Free of contagion from their boots.

Meet their misfortune with indifference,
God gives and takes with even hand,
Run from the heresies of difference,
Shun what you do not understand.

Stamp them like post, return to sender,
Keep them at bay with book and bell,
Make them conform, they must surrender
What they once were, and never tell.

Give them a begging bowl and offer
Just enough freedom to plead for alms,
Don't get too close, for fear you'll suffer
Contamination in their arms.

For this is not the holy water
Where Jordan's flood meets Galilee
And all our good resolves may falter
Before the river meets the sea.

St Leonard's lazar house, example
Of works of charity benign.
Now from each giver take a sample,
Ten sparks are human, one divine.

Though the unclean, always among us
Are objects of pity and suspicion,
Thanks to the crumbs which fate has flung us
We are not yet in their condition.

And as, at St Thomas Church, outsiders
Grasp at grace, the sermons hint
No space more distant, no chasm wider
Than that through which the lepers squint.

The Relics
St James the Great, Kilkhampton, June 23rd 2016

On the last night he locks away the relics;
Christ's likeness, bone of saint and mother's tear,
And thinks that this heresy and all its clerics
Will, like contagion, pass within the year.
He does not know the power of one day
To break the things he'd thought were made to last
And how those certainties are swept away
To the tantalising silence of the past.
That sound, translated, muddy as a field,
The crumbled ash of all that was divine,
The pledge from the shepherd to his flock, repealed,
The bread just bread, the red blood only wine.

Far, far away from his small round of duty;
Care for the relics, chalice, vestments, font,
The great ones, who care more for power than beauty,
Do not know what the little people want.
Where is the king? He's in his counting house
Where his will pounds the hammer to the nail,
Where are the faithful commons? They espouse
The truth, by proving that all men are frail.
Kings do not care to think about their souls
For they can bribe the angels at God's door,
While we, on thorny ground take up our bowls
And beg his intercession for the poor.

When he awakes, next day, he is aware
Of last night's pleas that God could not have heard,
That from this morning, when he kneels in prayer
Salvation can no longer be assured.
And while the little churches on the moor
Hunch against wind and weather, the unknown,
When we will not be Christ's people anymore,
Advances like a tide across the stone.
Looking again to where the darkness hovers,
A pestilence of fear behind the doubt,
How cold we are, he thinks and how uncovered,
When all the small, beloved lights go out.

Charmed Circle

In the hardware stores,
Which sprawl onto the pavements
In the backstreets of Athens,
Though mostly away from the monuments
Or the egg and bacon restaurants
Of the tourist quarter,
You can buy almost anything you need
For day to day survival.

There you will find a particular type of hook
For baiting eels,
Olive nets and rabbit traps,
Rubber cushions for old ladies' piles,
Ceramic lemon squeezers,
Sets of plastic clips
To secure your outdoor table cloths,
Tiny retsina glasses and copper coffee pots.

Near the back of the shop,
In the almost dark
Where a litter of orange cats
Are tangled by the stove,
Is a display of small brass plaques,
Hand sized and of uneven shape and thickness.
Stamped on to the metal, or hammered from a mould,
Is an anatomical image:

A foot or a leg, an ear, a hip, the fold of a neck,
A knee, an eye or a thumb.
Each little fetish is made
To be laid at the altar
Of any church, where the saint
Will intervene on your behalf.
Aghia Paraskevi, Aghios Georgios
And even Maria herself.

A couple of coins will buy you
A brazen intercession for any ailment,
From a wrenched knee to glaucoma,
From the ear that hears imperfectly
To the ankle that will no longer
Bear a worker's weight.
Some plaques are stamped with a circle
And balance a curled up baby inside.

Some carry a pile of coins by an empty wallet.
At the back of the display
One section sports a series of geometric parts,
From the round to the shrivelled
From the cartoon cursed
To the mortuary grotesque
The saints will ask the Christ, Pantocrator,
To mend your broken hearts.

Bells

We read them now, knowing what is to come,
Though they are still entirely innocent,
Inhabiting the pages of their ledgers
Oblivious to the blight of change which waits
At the coming of age of the century.

At the heart of all their business are the bells;
Two members to oil and to look after them
For twelve months at a time,
And paid at a salary of ten shillings each,
Subject to satisfactory attendance.

A set of very English proposals,
Each noted as unanimously carried;
Polite request for light in the belfry
And fortnightly oiling of the pulley pins,
To be put to the church warden.

A way of doing things, notes from another age;
Including from the rector, who hopes that in future
The ringers will stay for the sacred service
To which they have summoned the faithful,
Rather than ringing solely for pleasure.

Balance sheets to be read and passed
And thanks accorded for service,
Resignations accepted with regret
And fines imposed for lateness, subsequently used
To lighten the misfortunes of brother ringers.

Questions of change are seriously debated;
Castor oil to be used for a trial period,
The overhauling of the clappers,
The recitations in Lancashire dialect
Enjoyed at the annual picnic.

Their local names, repeated year to year
As secretary, Chairman, auditor and ringer,
Often through a lifetime's membership;
Wellens, Ogden, Hollows and Berry
Arrowsmith junior and senior, and Jacques.

The ringers' business, duly minuted,
Meeting to annual meeting logged
In a gentlemanly, post-Edwardian haze,
Before the calamity of war descends
Upon the sleepy parishes of England.

The Prayer Book Pilgrimage 1549

Even in darkness traces of light persist,
Though time wraps up the details in its shawl.
Pinpricks of intuition show up small.
Minutiae; like an ancient shopping list.
Item: The splash of surnames on a page.
Russell and Grenville, Raleigh, Drake, Carew.
The hundreds seethe, old order versus new
And fear is the language of change.

Item: The flash of colour from a stone
Set in a finger ring, upon a hand
Traveling across a page. Wet ink which damns
By signature alone.
Item: The snuff of wax, confounding doubt.
The flicker of a changing faith, spread thin,
Sealing the loyalties of new men in
And those of the faithful out.

Item: The stains of pitch upon the plaster,
Language burned from the lips, belief a fiction,
Splinters of colour, remnants of benediction,
Blank walls now overtaken by disaster.
Item: The crunch of boots upon the step,
The crash of brutal staves along the aisles,
The little saints all smashed upon the tiles
And how the sullen, stone-eyed people wept.

Item: The footprints to and from the gate
Where ritual offered time to break a fast
Where the old service shaped belief to last
And for the hungry even God would wait.
Footnote: the ragged Cornishmen who stand
Up from their country parishes to say
That they do not wish their comfort swept away
By words they can no longer understand.

A line of farmers, miners, fishermen
Who thought they would eat hog's pudding with the king,
Like sheaves of corn, just ripe for gathering
Cut down, their harvest never grown again.
And back in Lanson town, their ranks subdued
The men of Cornwall turn back to their task
Of just surviving, Cornish women ask
How many suffer for one old man's feud.

Item: the pale archbishop at his prayers,
Bent to his parchment, carves the mass anew.
Knowledge which lights a candle for the few,
The rest left in the dark to climb the stairs.
Item: the withered corn stalks in the field,
The nets un-mended in the fishing boats,
The wintry children wearing dead men's coats
Because their Cornish fathers would not yield.

Oh, When the Saints
St Peter-on-the-Wall, Bradwell-on-Sea

In those days
Everyone was doing it.
In fact it was quite a trend,
Amongst the younger children
Of better off families,
Who could afford to send
A couple of their kids
To be educated
At one of the new foundations.

And, at the end of every term,
There would be
Another cohort of apprentice
Would-be saints,
Trudging through mud and rain,
Converging on this cold little spit of land,
Whose craggy points
Rise up like pointing fingers
From the sea.

They climbed the cliff walls
And, burrowing
Through weird weather,
Planted their seedling faith
To be nurtured by the candles
And the climate
Until buds blossomed,
Fat and bursting with belief
Like litter in the hedgerows.

They watched the way
The light poured
From Old Testament clouds
Like streams of golden water
From God's slop bucket.
And, in that same flooding intensity,
Like an oncoming tide,
A line of saints
Marched down the coast of England.

Crossing from murky Iona
Turned East along the wall,
Then South to Lindisfarne
Or to the outpost at Whitby by way of
The rim of ocean
Which separated
That huddle of damp believers
From the founders
In sun-drenched Rome.

South and East they marched,
From outpost to drizzly outpost
Until they came to Bradwell,
Where St Peter-on-the-Wall
Looks out to sea
And where St Cedd, top of his class,
Built new illuminations
On top of the floundering darkness
Left behind.

Faith, like a lighthouse beam,
Stretched out one skinny digit
Over the stubbled corn
And lit a glisten of water.
Channels illumined, sliding
Amongst the salt marsh
And over samphire,
Spearing from the clay
Like a phalanx of Christian soldiers.

And there it still trembles,
Flaring amongst the shadows of the roof tiles
Where his ancient beam
Hangs even now, clinging wall to wall.
On a rare summer afternoon,
Just before tide-fall,
A company of Swallows swoop and swoon
Heathens at play, a tribe of native dissenters
Untroubled by belief.

Galilee

The Sunday crowd
Come swaggering down from the suburbs
To where the marshes
Absorb them into the salt flats,
Lunch them and launch them,
Sunbed-brown, tattooed and careless
Pouring the dregs of blueish jokes
Onto the placid water.

Jet skis cut to ribbons
The slow swell of the tide
And take shears to the rolling foam.
The blades of motor boats
Slice inlets of silence
Alongside the rumble of a sea tractor,
Bought from a man who knew a man
Who was once in the seafaring business.

Suddenly, a lacuna on the water,
There is a pool of quietness emerging.
Imagine a cloud descend and,
Out of time, palms stretched to keep his balance,
A man steps onto the waves,
Walks across from Mersea to Saint Lawrence,
Finger blessing the throng of revellers
Spilling their beer at the pub.

The shrill of oily gulls is muted,
Dazed into flocking silence
And white water trails in shock behind a boat
Which swerves to avoid him.
From the yacht club they watch through binoculars
Minuting how his gaze draws more obedience
Than their little book of rules
And litter bins spread out along the shore.

The Slapping birds float upwards
To roost in the tree tops,
Dogs snap their faces away from
Half flung sticks
To stare at the apparition.
Even the busy kayaks
Give way to the floating stillness
And wet-suited out-of-towners stop to gawp.

Everything stops
And tunes to radio silence.
There's not a chink of money at the bar.
A woman near the slip way, in red bikini,
Lowered to her knees,
Stage whispers to her husband
Gawd almighty! and you thought that only you
Could walk on water.

Carvery

In The George the Sunday lunchtime
Carvery is in full swing.
Joints of meat steam on the hotplate
Jewelled with sauce, like medieval bling.

Men with a rash from aftershave
Negotiate for extra meat,
Children, tense from good behaviour,
Kick the old peoples' chairs with hungry feet.

At the counter, octogenarians
Fill their plates with grim delight,
For all those weekends, unremembered,
Cannot damp their furious appetites.

On the news disaster rumbles,
Local pubs are in decline
But at The George the roast still tumbles,
Sliced and sanctified with flowing wine.

Enjoy the feast while plenty's lasting,
String life's pleasures on a thread,
While half the world is lost or fasting,
Sunday lunch will always raise the dead.

INDEFINITE

The Repentant Magdalene

His first woman,
Neither madonna nor mother,
Her flesh maternal, but those empty arms
Cradle only air.
As if they ached,
As if they ached
For a burden that was not there.

She frowns
At the space between her hands
Which have nothing to hold,
Fingers with no one to keep busy for.
As if the absent child is a gift
She has not earned,
She rocks the air to sleep.

Not languid
Nor longing, she squats
With her chin on her chest, she is
Foreshortened. She dozes
Dropped in a chair, his Magdalene told
To contemplate her lot.
Her penitence, exhaustion.

Flung from her
Lies a heap of discarded finery
Pulled from her neck.
The broken clasps of her profession.
How bare she is without them.
Her ears burn
With the sound of her own confession.

He knows her
Casually, as all who move in the artist's circle are known,
And he also knows her with his professional eye.
The seeing eye sees all.
Painted flesh will not be judged or forgiven,
The mirror he holds
Reflects but cannot recall.

A carafe
Of wine not drunk, now rancid
On her tongue, and on her brow
The pucker of a mark.
The unforgiving floor without relief,
The light of revelation out of reach,
Above her human dark.

Salome With the Head of John The Baptist

That platter has been hastily brought from the kitchens.
Snatched from a stack by the serving hatch,
Its scratches scoured as flat as the surface of a pool,
Reflecting its load
Of lavishly ripened fruit,
Or brace of exotic game
Or pyramid of bon-bons
Or a head with its tail in its mouth.

She carries that platter as if it held hot trotters,
Its steam rising to her nose and making her gag.
The towel keeps away the heat and the splatter
Of fat from her unstained hands.
All manner of savouries
Have been served to her.
She has been waited upon
But has never waited herself.

That platter is naked for the presentation,
While she is fully clothed and freshly ruffled, in sable,
New lace stitched into sleeves and throat. All veils
Swept under the table.
She is wearing a mourning black,
A uniform, waitress
Or execution black. A widow,
Black widow black.

And is she giving or is she receiving that platter?
A trophy for her mantlepiece. And is she properly flattered
By the assiduous speed with which her whim is granted?
She averts her face from his
Dear face, shorn in mid-prayer,
In righteous speech,
In righteous rejection and indifference.
His head will never turn to watch her dance.

The Supper at Emmaus

A stranger came to sit at our table,
Who ate our bread
As if it were food for kings.
A table bare of almost everything;
Rough loaf, oiled leaf,
A jug of Earthy wine,
A bowl of broth squeezed from the bone.
Beyond belief,
We brought a stranger home.

The linen laid, white turned yellow,
A cloth through which
The life already flowed.
No candle lit and yet that table glowed.
Hands meet.
Fingers bless and greet.
Nail to nail our shadows cross.
Palm to palm,
Leaves marks upon the cloth.

We talked and shared a dish
Of eggs and onions.
Goodman and wife,
Hot from the kitchen,
Used signs for words
We did not understand.
We called the neighbours, woke the street
To catch the crumbs
That scattered from a stranger's hand.

At night an extra place
Is always laid.
One plate is set aside,
One knife, one spoon,
One portion spare,
One chair, one prayer however poor,
Kept in reserve for any traveller
Who walks the Emmaus road
And is hungry at our door.

These Thanet Skies

A man high up on the cliff,
Under a brushed, broad brimmed top hat,
Brow squeezed in concentration.
Breathing light:
The fuel which guides his hand.
Numbed to all senses except sight,
Deaf to enquiries, however bland
As to health and weather and
Especially the artists' theme.
Only compelled to lay his paint
In thin, pale liquid rills which seem
To call up the sea and its reflected sky
In spray against the sand.

He walks there every day,
Stamping along the high paths after breakfast,
Eyeing his Kentish bay
Until the light drops stark behind the horizon,
And even later then, beyond the scarlet rising
Of the moon. On sudden stormy nights
He will continue flaying the canvass
Until the red rays, like a ship aground
And lumined to disaster,
Come creeping under the dark.
These Thanet skies
Are almost heavenly at dawn;
Cobalt, torn in an arc turned upside down.

He notices each wave's particular gloss,
Mauve as a plum on the incoming tide,
And how a fishing smack, precarious,
Weighed down with its silver catch
And listing to one side,
Plunges between viridian hills of water.
Behind it an ochre sunset explodes
Like the flare of a match,
And the roar of the air is liquid white
Against the black rind of the sea.
It creeps under his eyelids, a conflagration
Early in the morning
Until very late at night.

He wakes from dreams of deluge,
As inundation soaks his skin to crimson,
His flailing arms and scant breath
Hold him pinioned,
Like a Whale on a harpoon,
And slowly drag him down.
Hours and nightmares later he emerges,
A train from a tunnel,
Gasping for air, the colour of dawn engulfing
As a memory of birth,
Like the carcass of the fighting Temeraire,
Following the tugs as she is dragged
From water to rusty earth.

Turning back down the path,
His airy body returns to its earthly self
And asserts its requirements
Over the captured shadows and the air in flight.
His stiff boots strike a spark
Along the Margate cobbles
To where his own front door
Opens to streams of artificial light.
Bright candles, the smell of dinner
And the comfort of Mrs Booth
Who bathes the paint crust away and strokes
His concentrated rigid arms
Until they are light again and smooth.

Room Thirty-One

There are so many faces here,
Prised from the London streets,
Conducting this pilgrimage.
Some are from offices nearby,
Taking advantage
Of a cancelled meeting,
Or squeezing in a breather after lunch.
Others spill off the bus,
To make a casual visit, just for fun.
Others still, who made the trek
From somewhere far away
Across the world,
Wash up at room thirty-one.

Fragments of languages,
Some chattering with knowledge, some in awe,
All peering at the faces on the wall
Who stare straight back.
This babel space is crammed with onlookers
Who come to peep at shadows
Of sleekly muscled saints,
Popes in regalia,
Exuding both humility and love,
Or some forgotten dignitary
Who got himself painted
Under the revelation of the spirit
Represented by a dove.

Their four centuries' old gaze
Is unsettlingly direct.
They strike a sense of tiptoe,
Self-imposed. The soundless foot on floor,
Along with the hush of foreign sibilance,
As if we were all born
Knowing to step more quietly in a gallery,
And reverent, as if in church.
A child confounds the rule,
Dropping his half-eaten apple
On the polished floor, howling for its return,
Being hushed by a guard
In benign disapproval.

Jesus is, as ever, unperturbed,
His hand stretched out toward us,
Blessing us watching
From our fairground mirror.
Perspective distorts the angle,
A half a thousand years ago depiction
Of an act far older than that.
We know the story behind
The most famous painting in the room.
The astonished disciples, listening landlord
And the dead man, the saviour,
Suddenly undisguised,
And newly arrived from the tomb.

The miracles are hung along the wall,
Its green flock soothing
Successive shocks of colour.
The pictures suspended on chains,
The blue skied allegories
With their vanishing points
Each captured as a moment.
The Baptist's head on its plate,
A dead Roman washed up on a beach,
And Thomas's doubting finger,
Pink cheeked Europa on her bull,
And all around her little cherubs
Flutter, just out of reach.

Why do we all come here?
All of us quotidian courtiers
Who pace the gallery floor?
Unconcerned with brushstrokes
Or information inscribed upon a plaque
But viewing with relief the worn-out stories
Told in paint to reassure.
Concerned instead with authentication
And to show that you were really here, you offer
The selfie in front of Caravaggio
Where, be-denimmed and with your hair just so
And sporting an art lovers smile, in the know,
You have been invited to supper.

What is most astonishing
Is the resemblance
Between the then and now,
And how the pugilistic man
With a boxer's flattened nose
Who is staring at John's decapitated head,
Looks somehow familiar.
He is a regular on canvass,
He has been here before,
As has the girl with the revolted sneer,
And the crone with crooked fingers,
Two surprised oldish men and even Jesus himself,
We've all been here before.

CHEF JESUS
Berkeley Church

There's only a little bit of Jesus left.
Alpha and Omega: his right hand
Reaches out
And from the stump
Fall all those little souls
Dispatched below.
In crumbled masonry, his face awry,
And sweating like flakey pastry,
He swallows them whole, they are
The filling for his pie.

His justice is dispensed: a weight of flour
Poured through time's sieve.
One penitent still waits,
Hovering behind him on the ceiling,
Last diner in the restaurant.
All those stars
Are just a remnant now, as old
And stale as yesterday's bread.
Doom is obscured, gone off the boil,
It's urgency grown cold.

Chef Jesus has been cooking here
For a scant thousand years,
Stewing his stock-pot brew
Damnation strong and hot
As Hell's kitchen.
Walls stained the colour of meat.
Frowning, his stern appetites ablaze,
He hangs, quite filleted, above the rood screen
With all his savage recipes forgotten
And all his red ingredients erased.

The Twelve

Here we are crammed,
A dozen strangers trying to understand
The grimy trail of other peoples' lives.
People like us, whose daily underhand
Will help us to determine
What makes a moment's madness.

It is a significant number;
The months of the year,
Tied to their human rhythm.
The twelve in an upstairs room, all angry,
All in agreement, except one;
The asker of awkward questions.

We are reluctant
To end our deliberation
And enter transition from flux to fixity.
For we are just strangers,
Bombarded with detail
And paralysed by our own ineptitude.

A drawer is opened,
Laid out for our inspection:
Minutiae so raw and so mundane,
Personal items to handle, somewhat stained.
Our rictus fingers lock behind our backs
The shock so intimate we have to look away.

The question being asked:
Did her bloodstained knickers
Come off voluntarily?
Is the message on her telephone an actual threat
Or just an everyday brutal endearment?
Did she really believe her life was in danger?

Overawed with possibility,
Oh let us prevaricate for just
A few minutes longer.
Someone's life will be changed by us,
We have become, if not God,
At least somewhat angelic.

St Peter is already at the gate,
Holding the scroll of works and days
By which to calculate the worth
Of someone not ourselves.
Have we felt that? Have we done that?
Seen that? Said that? Thought that?

Could we have also fallen so far beneath
The measure of what can be forgiven?
Here we sit, twelve strangers
Trying to understand
The depths of other peoples' hearts,
While barely afloat in the shallows of our own.

INFINITE

A Song of Parting
(For those who meet and say goodbye at stations)

The day they peeled the bells for us at Nibley
And both our mothers said they wouldn't come,
I brought you home from Stinchcombe Hill to Wickwar
Uncaring of their disapproving tongues.

Sheep hugged the shade, the heads of horses hanging,
The house a lump of butter on the hill.
You cried at the tangle of the kitchen garden
But I can taste your mint and parsley still.

We'd climb from the halt at Golden Valley:
Cam Peak, Long Down, our house tucked up so small.
And how we laughed at the smuts upon the washing.
From Tyndale Hill you can see all.

You opened the eyes of daisies at the station,
Conjured teasles, poppies and red Loosestrife.
How blessed with your beauty I have been
The many hundred mornings of my life.

How the stories of people who wait for trains,
The overheard, the snatched or underhand
Would move you with the joyfulness of living,
A bunch of flowers unfreezing in your hand.

I watch us tell the story of your going,
Smooth as a hankie laid across the sun,
I watch you with a child's sense of shrinking,
The long, long days of waiting almost done.

Deep down in the belly of this last summer,
Glimpsed from windows where commuters peep,
Two old people in deck-chairs in their garden,
One gone, the other waits to go to sleep.

At the Crumbly Edge of Empire

When I was young and married
We used to travel slow,
From Nairobi to Mombasa
Where the game and sunsets glow.
The zebra and the vague giraffe
Of fifty years ago.

It's a cold dawn, so keep warm and do not cry.
For there's blue, blue in the very, very green red sky.
Mother will come from far away to give us tea.
There's the shrill sound of being young
And the smell of the sea,
The smell of the sea.

From Petersburg to Riga,
And light's sparkle in Tallinn,
The sun was a disk in the frozen sky
When we came breathless in
And a slope-backed peasant swore at me
From his stubbled chin.

It's a cold dawn, so keep warm and do not cry
For there's blue, blue in the very, very green red sky.
Mother will come from far away to give us tea,
There's the shrill sound of being young
And the smell of the sea,
The smell of the sea.

I travelled from Agra to Puri,
A coastal town,
When a hoard full of hate, a fury,
Came sweeping down.
They hoisted a hundred people
And then they cut them down.

It's a cold dawn, so keep warm and do not cry,
For there's blue, blue in the very, very green red sky,
Mother will come from far away to give us tea,
There's the shrill sound of being young
And the smell of the sea
The smell of the sea.

Seventy-Nine Bench Ends
St Nonna's Church, Altarnun

He crouches on a workman's stool
And holds the slab between his knees;
Dark oak, on which, with cutters' tools,
He carves the pictures that he sees

Beginning with the everyday.
The blackened wood retreats to peel
The figures, names now stripped away,
Just their humanity revealed.

A man, in winter coat and britches,
No arms nor title can he bring,
There is no sign of wealth or riches,
Only his dog pulled on a string.

Here grins the jester at misrule
And the motley that he wears
Shows, in the parti-coloured fool,
The black and white of man, still there.

Here are the fiddles and the pipes,
The bowls and platters of rough clay,
And, as the fields are carved in stripes
He carves the harvest of the day.

Amongst the pews the pictures grow
Of wounds upon God's hands and feet,
And where the benches end, a row
Of mermaids and archangels meet.

The children come to watch him work
And in good time they bring their own.
Within the little church the spark
Of candles light what they have known.

The carpenter sits at his door
And all around him shavings lay.
He knows the Greene man of the poor,
That man, in turn, knows Robart Daye.

He cuts the letters of his name
With his sharp chisel on the wood.
My fingers blindly trace the same,
Five hundred years from where he stood.

THE WOMEN WHO SHAPED THE CHURCH
St Materiana's Church at Tintagel

To read about them
In the footnotes of church history,
Often in the individual pamphlets
So thoughtfully provided,
You would have expected that those early saints,
Young women with wispy hairdos and strange names
Traipsing up and down the country lanes,
Establishing their pilgrim routes,
Would have, at least occasionally collided.

Many were from the same family,
Siblings, the children of converted kings,
Or even at times a single person
With a variety of pseudonyms.
It can't have been easy, introducing a whole religion
Whose stories so clearly came
From a hot foreign country
Into this rocky, damp, suspicious island
Far out on its Cornish limb.

But those women were indefatigable,
Materiana, Nonna and Morwenna.
Perhaps the only other choice, being marriage,
To grumpy local chiefs of dubious reputation,
Made the rigours of evangelism a favourable prospect.
When they met up, to celebrate their successes
Or for one another's birthdays
They will have exchanged tokens of encouragement
And advice on winning over the local population.

And how do you know the right place to found a church?
Do you just sit down at the side of a road
With your tatty old carpet bags
Bursting with biblical verses
And let the local villagers
Build an anchorage around you?
Or do you bustle from town to town performing miracles,
Arranging fetes and drumming up volunteers
To sink foundations quickly, before the novelty disperses.

Imagine them stumbling,
Through rain as thick as stair rods,
The clog of clay in their shoes,
The potholes miring every step, hungry and discontented,
And how at the end of another day of nobody listening
They thought of returning to their families,
To the hot stews and sturdy castle walls,
And giving up all thought of Heaven
Which after all, was only just invented.

And I wonder what stopped them
Throwing in the towel.
Visions and dreams, moments of clarity,
A wink to posterity or stubborn faith alone?
Perhaps there was a whisper on God's bush telegraph,
Of what each other was doing.
How the stout little church on Tintagel cliff was finished
And how that silent graveyard over the sea
Boasted its first believers under stone.

Perhaps they left signs for each other,
A cruciform configuration of sticks,
A scrawled blessing, or pot of tea shop jam.
A verse hacked onto a milestone at night
In indecipherable script, bleached windy white.
Across the lanes and coves and cliffs
These smiling ladies still trudge to and fro
With their heavy bags and their heavy boots
And their faith to make them light.

Salvage
St Morwenna's at Morwenstowe

Each night he dreams that he is drowning,
Water clasps him and he fears
His Lord is not benign; God's frown
Blows tempests in his eyes and ears.

Reverend Hawker, sleeps but poorly,
Twisting the linens on his bed
Thinks that on this occasion, surely
Someone else can raise the dead.

From the church his moonlit strides
Trace the familiar path, the meadows
Call him to where the cliff top hides,
A beacon crouched amongst the shadows,

From where he sits, the tides which boom
Along the shoreline's ragged edge
Echo upwards to the room
Which he has carved upon the ledge.

There he sits with pen and paper
Jotting thoughts like candle sparks
Weaving the fronds of faith which waver
For tomorrow's sermon marks.

There on the cliff his God seems nearer
Up there the angel voices hang,
Away from the Trumpets which deafen the hearer
With the waves' overwhelming clang.

Whilst the storm winds rage, emphatic,
Black land looms on the horizon
Reverend Hawker, charismatic,
Whispers a Kyrie Eleison.

Down on the beach with rope and sacking
Hauling drowned men through the ferns,
Up past the rocks, with hope unpacking,
Back to his church where a candle burns.

He keeps the tally like God's banker,
Invests their hopes in holy ground,
Gives the young men of the ships an anchor;
He is the haven for the drowned.

After the storm has mauled its quarry,
After the crew has sunk below
After the dawn has murmured sorry
Sun rays fall on Morwenstowe.

CHING ALLEY
St Mary Magdalene Launceston

And was there not one of them
That had thought
That these were God's gifts
For them to save and nurture,
To woo back to thankful health,
To speak of as saviours,
To adopt, to rescue and to court
Rather than speculate that luck
Or fate or God had thrown up
This catch of human fish
To do with as they liked,
For their pleasure
Or for sport?

He could not un-know the detail
Although he will not tell his wife
The forensic evidence
Which pales like a bleached twig
Before her grief for the fact.
That her son,
Whose heart had known nothing
But hope and humour
And was scoured by a sense
Of human decency
Should meet, at the end
Such a barrage of unthinking cruelty,
In such a brutal act.

Ignorant savages he called them,
Even then unable to call them evil
Any more than the sea itself is evil.
Untamed, untutored, unredeemed
Unmindful of the light.
His son's killers
Only worthy of pity,
Before the strong voice of God's own son
Who prayed, forgive them father
What could he do but acquiesce
And lay a brass marker at the church's door?
Just another father who lost his boy
And had no continuing city.

Ralph

Soon the forsythia
Will appear again
In full Spring regalia:
Yellow spangles of blossom
Spreading on brown twig arms,
Before a hint of leaf becomes apparent.
You won't see it this year,
Being too busy with dying,
But you may have had time to notice
That the branches were still bare
And you knew, or at least believed
In the coming rejuvenation,
Even though you could not
Wait for it yourself.

Next comes the clematis,
As contagious as a rash,
Every tendril itchy with it
Until the whole bushy lattice
Is awash with erupting colour
And stained embroidery pink.
But you won't feel its scratch this year,
I imagine the little trees on the lane
Outside your empty house
Are still bare shouldered,
Wearing their end of winter nudity.
Even on the last morning
You might still have laughed
To think of the trees as girls.

When I last looked out at the garden,
I had not heard your news
And watched, as yet unsaddened
As a small, pale primrose
Unfolded on the lawn
And the not-yet-quite-red tulips
Stretched their blind green leaves
Up to the almost sun.
By then you had already turned your head,
Too far away to mind
The buds on our pear tree.
They are hardly there yet,
But getting themselves ready
For the Spring you have already left behind.

The Hurlers

There's a circle of stones at Minions Moor
That was once a circle of men,
But they played too hard in God's back yard
And they couldn't go home again.

The call went round in the morning,
As they straggled to Church to pray
And talk of the prize they'd take home to their wives
Persuaded the team to play.

The challenge rang out in the village
Though the vicar shook his head
Better stay poor and obey God's law
Than anger him, he said.

But the Captain smiled into the Eucharist cup
And his teammates did the same,
We've worked like drones and the harvest's home,
He'll not begrudge our game.

And they did not know, as the game began,
With the flex of flesh and bone
That by the first gong of Evensong
They'd be struck as still as stone.

Oh who would have guessed that a wooden ball
And a kit bag over the shoulder
And a heart as light as a kestrel's flight
Could have grown to weigh a boulder.

But the Lord is a fierce master
And severe as a ten-foot tide
And men at play on a holy day
Is a leisure he can't abide.

It isn't true said the relatives,
Our God wouldn't be unkind,
His laws aren't meant for punishment
But only to remind.

And is that what he told the Pipers
Who were petrified at his glance?
Or the merry maids at St Buryan, stayed
In their perfect circle dance?

There's the sudden surprise of insight
And the rush of the moor's own cold;
The bone deep chill on the windy hill
As the flint of his will takes hold.

They crouch in their standing circle
Like players in mid-game
And although the law has obscured the score
The questions remain the same.

What secrets has a stone man?
What lies can his stone mouth tell?
Does he show surprise in his granite eyes?
Does his stone-sense catch our smell?

They stand quite still on the dripping moor
Attuned to its lash of sound,
But they do not hear us creeping near
As the silent years grind round.

The moss creeps over the hurlers
And their features are scoured and smooth,
They took their name for a Sunday game
Of which God did not approve.

Have pity on all statues
Whose hopes have turned to clay
And remember them as breathing men
As their faces crumble away.

Unborn Chicks

We are not here.
You do not need to miss us,
There is no stone
That you can lay to remember
Those you have never known.

We are the never-happened
And un-numbered.
Our unimagined ranks,
Village-on-village absent
Deaf to thanks.

We did not have potential
Nobody ever asked
Who might have been.
Undreamed of, uncreated
And unseen.

We are not mourned
As those who were lost
Are mourned.
We are not dead
But only the unborn.

Worthy

Here lies Sir Henry Newton, Knight,
Upon his chilly bed of stone,
Beside him Katherine, out of sight,
Waits quietly, as she's always done.

His leather surcoat, scuffed with years,
Is belted, buckled, braced to serve,
His sword lies ready, and his beard
Is trimmed and neat, his air reserved.

Around his neck a ruff, new-starched,
His pillow, never creased by sleep,
Above him, dreams of duty arch,
His stony eyes a vigil keep.

Beneath him, on the monument,
His sons and daughters kneel in rows,
Two boys, his marble replicas,
Four little girls who never grow.

Titles and coats of arms surround him,
Lilies, leopards disappearing,
Worthy honours crumble round him,
Tourists ignore him within hearing.

One hand lies quietly on his heart,
Swearing to purity of life.
We cannot see the other hand
Which, must, for comfort, clutch his wife's.

Momentarily

Some moments are dense as forests,
Overhung, with the premature sense of future recall,
Drops of water, cast like runes, revealing all
And trapped on the skin of a leaf.
Others disperse and scatter; time at play,
Perfectly unmemorable, after the fact,
And already pouring away.

This is how life passes,
The ever-present motor of what if,
Emptied, like a cataract over a cliff.
And we cannot preserve
A single second, other than through a surge
Of purpose within the mechanics of our senses,
However acute the urge.

Next door an anxious dog
Howls her present grief, memory already burned,
She has misplaced her faith that her people will return.
But now, in this moment of extremity,
Of pressing loneliness, however brief,
She cannot summon the knowledge
To comfort her disbelief.

Do the bees remember the flowers in pollen?
Or is each encounter newly resonant, striking a chime
Of recognition on the hour, each for the very first time?
Does the warm bench
Remember the sun on its timber
And recall the departed luxury of summer
Even in winter?

And in the garden now, this very minute,
Where the rose hips are suddenly bright and shining red,
And the purple curl of buddleia not quite dead,
Where one branch of dusty apples
Hangs over the wall where the blown, brown roses stand,
I sit and watch this delicate old summer
Play out her final hand.

This silent, golden afternoon
Interrupted by the gilded tinkle of childhood pleasure,
An Italian out of tune, Ice cream van's measure,
Somewhere at the top of Angel Hill.
And I wonder if, in the future, if ever, if at all,
I try to remember a perfect moment
It will be this one I recall.

Notes to the Poems

These poems, written at many different junctures and for a variety of projects seem to me to have a single theme; faith. Not all of them are concerned with the kinds of faith which might be contained by religion or ideas of God and some are more preoccupied with our ideas of faith in ourselves and our own humanity or lack of it.

The division of the poems into three sections was devised by my colleague and close friend Chris Salt who, like me studied theology for a while and felt that the reader might experience the poems in a very particular, almost grammatically precise way. Within these divisions the definite become a phenomenon experienced at first hand and the indefinite one mediated through a work of art or a tale told by somebody else. I like the addition of the infinite to the definite and indefinite article as if some ideas are bigger and last longer than their parts.

Some poems in the collection are very much linked to place and some again are parts of sequences inspired by a particular location. *At the Cathedral* and *Worthy* which bookend the anthology depict the architecture and monuments in Bristol Cathedral while *The Twelve* was composed during a term of Jury Service at the city's Magistrate's Court.

Chef Jesus was composed during a visit to the Chapel at Berkely in Gloucestershire in response to the doom painting which can still be seen in fragments on the wall. The piece subsequently appeared as a lyric in the libretto for *The Bargees Wife* commissioned for the 2013 3 choirs festival at Gloucester Cathedral and written with composer John O'Hara.

Charmed Circle recreates the interior of an Athenian hardware shop in the 1980s. These little talismans are still found placed underneath an icon at many remote Orthodox churches.

Bells was written for the exhibition *A Cargo of Curiosities for Edgeways Productions* at Alkrington Hall, Manchester in 2016 and is based on the minutes of the bell ringers society archive preserved at Middleton Church.

The first three poems in section two are responses to Caravaggio paintings for an in-progress song-cycle composition with composer Thomas Johnson. *Salome with the Head of John The Baptist* and *The Supper at Emmaus* both hang in Room 31 of the National Gallery in London. *These Thanet skies* was written in response to a visit to the Turner Contemporary Gallery in Margate where Turner's own diary entry describing *These Thanet Skies* as the widest in Europe is quoted above the entrance. *Room Thirty-One* was written while visiting the Caravaggio paintings in Room 31 of the National Gallery in London.

The Poems whose titles are followed by Cornish church locations were written during a three-month residency at Charles Causley's house, Cypress Well in Launceston during the summer of 2016, supported by the Charles Causley Trust and Arts Council England. The little churches in and around Launceston and Bodmin became the focus of my attention as an antidote to the Brexit campaign.

Altarnun Church of St Nonna is known as the Cathedral of the Moor and the meticulously polished and preserved Tudor bench ends there are internationally famous. *Ching Alley* was written in response to the very moving memorial to John Ching, who was lost to a cannibalistic attack having been shipwrecked on an island in the south China Seas in 1834. The memorial stone was commissioned by his father in St Mary Magdalene Church and Ching Alley itself also commemorates the young man in the town.

The legends of the Reverend Hawker's hut at Morwenstowe and The Leper squint at St Thomas's where Charles Causley is buried are based on local history notes in the church pamphlets. Hawker's hut was carved by the Reverend himself out of the cliff face and furnished with a bench and a heavy door where he could sit out the frequent storms. The land mass visible from the cliff is Lundy Island. The hut is now covered with tiny pieces of graffiti made by visitors from all over the world. The Leper Squint was an iron grille at the far end of the church through which members of the local leper colony could observe the service without being part of the congregation.

The Hurlers at Minion's Moor, like the Merry Maidens at St Buryans, are archaeological sites of standing stone circles, said to have been villagers petrified at God's displeasure. *The Pilgrimage of Grace* was my response to reading A.L Rowse's *Tudor Cornwall: Portrait of a Society. Carvery,* was also written in Launceston during a solitary meal at the George pub in the town. Eating at the Carvery was one of Charles Causley's favourite treats.

Ralph was written to commemorate a friend, Ralph De Jong Mellon who died on March 1st 2019.

The first two poems of the third section were written during a devising project for a song-cycle written with composer Thomas Johnson as part of the Arts council of England's Year of the Artist scheme. Composer and librettist spent a month on the small train which plies between Bristol and Gloucester creating a song, through verbatim encounters with fellow passengers, for each station along the route These two particular poems represented the station at Cam and Dursley and the one at Yate.

The poems entitled *Galilee* and *Oh When the saints* were written during a trip to St Lawrence on the Essex marshes during the summer of 2019. St Peter-on-the-wall is one of the oldest extant Christian foundations in the country dating from the 6th century.

Unborn Chicks was written as part of an Oratorio *The Street of Bugles* with composer Tom Johnson but never made it into the finished piece. It was a contribution to the WW1 centenary memorials funded by the Heritage Lottery taking place across the country to commemorate the Great War.

The last poem in the collection *Momentarily* was written on the very last afternoon of a three-month residency at Cypress Well.

The Author

Karen Hayes first full collection, *The Houses Along the Wall – a Pembrokeshire poetry cycle*, was published by Holland Park Press in 2018.

Karen spent the early part of her working life as an actor and musician and became an ensemble member and lyricist and later artistic director of the Bristol-based theatre collective Public Parts.

She moved towards poetry, lyric and libretto writing and creating verbatim texts with marginalised groups. She has produced two anthologies about living with aspects of dementia.

I Had an Angel, written with composer John O'Hara, was produced live and as an opera film for WNO. *The Bargee's Wife,* also written with John O'Hara, was produced for the 3 Choirs Festival.

Her libretto for composer Thomas Johnson's *The Street of Bugles* which was performed at the 3 Choirs Festival and a cycle of poetry to accompany an arts installation *A Cargo of Curiosities* with film-maker Chris Salt.

She was Charles Causley poet-in-residence at Cypress Well in 2016. In 2017, her poem *The Belgians* won the Foreign Voices competition.

More information is available from
http://www.hollandparkpress.co.uk/authors/karen-hayes/

Holland Park Press, founded in 2009, is a privately-owned independent company publishing literary fiction: novels, novellas, short stories; and poetry. The company is run by brother and sister team Arnold and Bernadette Jansen op de Haar, who publish an author not just a book. Holland Park Press specialises in finding new literary talent by accepting unsolicited manuscripts from authors all year round and by running competitions. It has been successful in giving older authors a chance to make their debut and in raising the profile of Dutch authors in translation.

To

Learn more about Karen Hayes
Discover other interesting books
Read our unique Anglo-Dutch magazine
Find out how to submit your manuscript
Take part in one of our competitions

Visit www.hollandparkpress.co.uk

Bookshop: http://www.hollandparkpress.co.uk/books.php

Holland Park Press in the social media:

http://www.twitter.com/HollandParkPres
http://www.facebook.com/HollandParkPress
http://www.linkedin.com/company/holland-park-press
http://www.youtube.com/user/HollandParkPress
http://www.instagram.com/hollandparkpress/